Reading Journal Response for Grades Pre-K–5

by Karen Soll

Gail Saunders-Smith, PhD, consulting editor

capstone classroom

Capstone Classroom
1710 Roe Crest Drive,
North Mankato, Minnesota 56003
www.capstoneclassroom.com

Copyright © 2015 by Capstone Classroom, a division of Capstone.

All rights reserved. No part of this publication may be reproduced in whole or in part, or stored in a retrieval system, or transmitted in any form or by any means, electronic, mechanical, photocopying, recording, or otherwise, without written permission of the publisher. For information regarding permission, write to Capstone Classroom, 1710 Roe Crest Drive, North Mankato, Minnesota 56003.

Reading Journal Response for Grades Pre-K-5
by Karen Soll

978-1-62521-957-2

Cover and Book Design: Jodi Pedersen

Cover art from Shutterstock

Table of Contents

INTRODUCTION 4
JOURNAL RESPONSES 5
    My favorite part was 5
    Here is a picture of my favorite part 6
    I liked/didn't like this book because 7
    This book is about. 8
    One part I would rewrite is. 9
    I thought the author did a good job of. 10
    I would/would not recommend this book to others because 11
    An important event that happened in this book was 12
    If I were one of the characters, I would have 13
    If I were alive during that time, I would have. 14
    If I could communicate. 15
    If I could meet the person. 16
    A list of descriptions that I like in the book are 17
    Something I learned about science 18
    Something I learned about the past is 19
    Two characters or events can be compared. They are. 20
    One event or person caused another. 21
    This genre of this book is. 22
    This book reminds me of 23
JOURNAL RESPONSE LOG 24

Introduction

A child's connection to reading can be strengthened with a short writing activity after a book has been read. This book includes several journal responses from which to choose. The responses may be used with nonfiction or fiction and may even be adapted for poetry and plays. Select the journal response that is most appropriate, and give your child time to write a short response to the prompt.

If your child is struggling to come up with a response, ask specific questions. For example, with the journal response that asks why you didn't like the book, you could say, "I remember you frowned when I read about ... Did that part bother you?"

If your child is a reluctant writer, here are some quick tips you could try:

- Hold the pen while your child tells you what he or she would like to write. Sound out the words as you write the letters.
- Sound out the letters as your child is writing the words.
- Ask your child questions that may help him or her write the answer.
- Ask your child to connect the book to his or her life and ask how.
- Allow your child to use the computer to respond.

Help make the writing activity enjoyable by allowing your child to respond to whatever he or she related to. When reviewing your child's work, respond to the content of his or her writing rather than the mechanical errors. Journal writing should be viewed as a quick, fun way to give an opinion or extend the learning.

A log has been included at the end of this guide. We recommend that you fill it in whenever your child responds to a text.

Journal Response

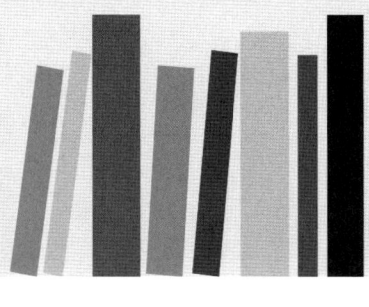

Title of Book _____ Date _____

My favorite part was ...

Journal Response

Title of Book _____ Date _____

Here is a picture of my favorite part.

Journal Response

Title of Book _____ Date _____

I liked/didn't like this book because ...

Journal Response

Title of Book _____ Date _____

This book is about ...

Journal Response

Title of Book _____ Date _____

One part I would rewrite is ...

Journal Response

Title of Book _____ Date _____

I thought the author did a good job of ...

Journal Response

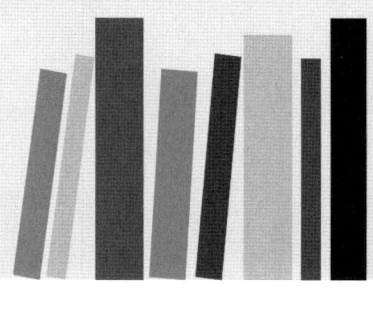

Title of Book _____ Date _____

I would/would not recommend this book to others because …

Journal Response

Title of Book _____ Date _____

An important event that happened in this book was ...

Journal Response

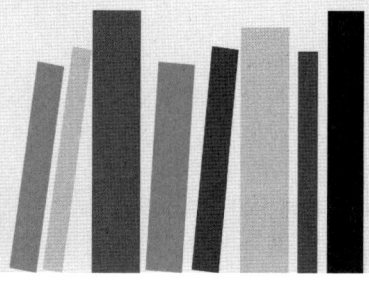

Title of Book _____ Date _____

If I were one of the characters, I would have ...

Journal Response

Title of Book _____ Date _____

If I were alive during that time, I would have ...

Journal Response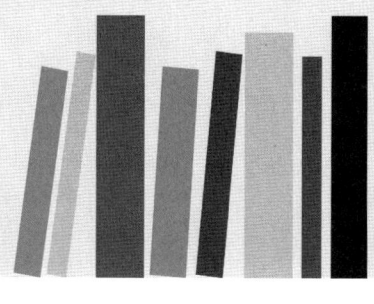

Title of Book _____ Date _____

If I could communicate with the people of the time or the characters, I would have said …

Journal Response

Title of Book _____ Date _____

If I could meet the person in this biography, I would ask …

Journal Response

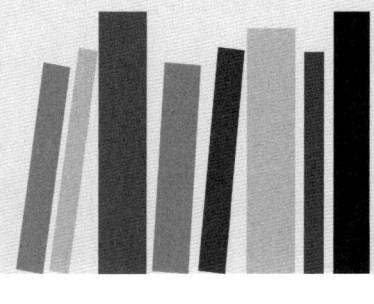

Title of Book _____ Date _____

A list of descriptions that I like in the book are ...

I like them because ...

Journal Response

Title of Book _____ Date _____

Something I learned about science from reading this book is ...

Journal Response

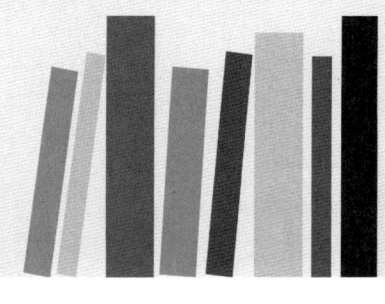

Title of Book _____ Date _____

Something I learned about the past is ...

Journal Response

Title of Book _____ Date _____

Two characters or events can be compared.
They are ...

Journal Response

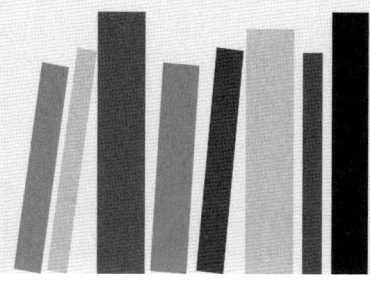

Title of Book _____   Date _____

One event or person in the book caused another event to happen. It is ...

Journal Response

Title of Book _____ Date _____

This genre of this book is _____

I know because ...

Journal Response

Title of Book _____ Date _____

This book reminds me of ...

Journal Response Log

Date	Title of Book	Response